ROADWAY TO SUCCESS

(Let Go and Let God)

Poems
with Inspirational Explanations

Georgia E. Wells

Resurrection Life Publications
Temple Hills, Md 20757

ISBN 0-9706160-0-7

Library of Congress Control Number 2002091617

Cover photo by Deacon Anthony K. Wells, SR.

Edited by
Minister Ann C. Connor
Minister Tarika J. Robinson

Published by Resurrection Life Publications
P.O. Box 1644
Temple Hills, MD 20757
301-452-2618
e-mail: geewells@akwells.com

Printed in the United States of America

TABLE OF CONTENTS

Struggles

Inspiration

References

DEDICATION

This book is dedicated to those who are hurting and holding on to pain. Holding pain inside, and nursing and rehearsing it, prolongs the pain. Release the person and the pain, and continue with your life. Do not make pain and those who cause it a god.

ACKNOWLEDGMENTS

I thank my husband Anthony and my daughter Renee' for encouraging me as I penned the words to this book to bless you, the readers, in your walk through life. I commend their patience as they allowed me space to perfect this work.

I acknowledge my pastor, Minister Bobby D. Hicks, of New Home Baptist Church, who encourages us to dream, and demands that we teach and preach sound doctrine.

I thank Ministers Ann Connor and Tarika Robinson for editorial services. I also thank Deacon Bernard Blunt for assistance with the cover and other areas.

I thank God for His grace, mercy, love and forgiveness of my shortcomings.

PREFACE

This book is a medley of poems expressing what I was experiencing at the time of the writing or what inspired me to pen the poems. Each poem contains a write-up with words of deliverance, encouragement, and inspiration for the reader. I know you will find comfort in this book as well as be challenged to change.

The poems start with struggles which every individual will experience. How we handle our struggles determines our victory or our defeat.

There are also poems pointing to the power of God and the inspirations of others because of what God has done in their life.

Within this book are principles of deliverance that will help you get beyond yourself and see the power of God moving in your life. Often times we fail to reach our potential in God because of roadblocks in our lives. Deliverance is necessary in many instances to bring us to the point where we can see God and experience His fullness. You do not have to stay in bondage. Let this book show you the RoadWay to Success.

FINDING JOY IN YOUR SEASONS

There are seasons in our lives and Solomon explains that, *To every thing there is a season, and a time to every purpose under the heaven:* (Ecclesiastes 3:1). He explains in detail in Ecclesiastes 3:1-8 the times for everything under the sun which includes times of good and bad. Whatever the season, we must find joy. There will be times of trials and tribulations but they are for a season. This means they will come and go. How we handle these trials and tribulations determines whether we find joy in the midst of our pain. The scripture says, *Then he said unto them, Go your way, eat the fat, and drink the sweet, and send portions unto them for whom nothing is prepared: for this day is holy unto our Lord: neither be ye sorry; for the joy of the LORD is your strength* (Nehemiah 8:10).

When trials and tribulations come, it is the Lord that brings us through. He gives us joy in the midst of our suffering. Paul says, *Rejoice in the Lord alway: and again I say, Rejoice* (Philippians 4:4). The joy of the Lord has healing medicine that will give us strength to endure. Jesus endured the death of the cross based on the joy set before Him. This proves that joy gives us strength. It enhances our faith that God has our situation in control. This joy helps us to know that if Jesus chooses to delay or deny reprieve, He will give us peace in the midst of the pain. Stop whining, crying, and complaining for it only makes us more miserable. We must trust God to handle our problems.

Joy is also one of the fruit of the Spirit. It come from God and is given to his children for strength. We, as Christians, are an example to the world of the joy found in knowing Jesus.

We must trust God in our dark season as well as in our good season. God is faithful. Paul writes that, *There hath no temptation taken you but such as is common to man: but God is faithful, who will not suffer you to be tempted above that ye are* able; but will with the temptation also make a way to escape, that ye may be able to bear it (1 Corinthians 10:13).   Let us trust God that whatever trials and tribulations we are going through, that He will not leave us in the situation but bring us out. The key phrase is going through. We are not living in the problem, but moving from the problem to victory. Remember that... *weeping may endure for a night, but joy cometh in the morning* (Psalm 30:5).

We are God's children and we must be rooted and grounded in Him. If we are abiding in Jesus, we have confidence that, as we go through, we can call on Him. We also know that He hears us and will respond in due time. Remember, He is never late!

If we recognize the greatness of God, it will gives us strength to go through. It will gives us strength to let go of the doubts, insecurities, conflicts, and struggles, and to allow God to perfect His will in us.

The purpose of this writing is to help us understand that the God of the morning is also the God of the night and He will bring us through the pain and fear of the night.

Trust in the LORD with all thine heart; and lean not unto thine own understanding. In all thy ways acknowledge him, and he shall direct thy paths. Proverbs 3:5-6

UNCERTAINTY

I count my options
Where do I belong?
To the right or to the left,
Where do I go?

I thought I knew the direction
But I lost it along the way.
To the right or to the left,
Which way do I go?

Tomorrow is another day
Do I make my decision then?
But yesterday was tomorrow
Yet no decision has been made.

Today is the time for decision
I must stop procrastinating.
To the right or to the left,
Which way do I go?

There are many crossroads in life. When we get to them, which way do we go? Jesus says, *For which of you, intending to build a tower, sitteth not down first, and counteth the cost, whether he have sufficient to finish it? Lest haply, after he hath laid the foundation, and is not able to finish it, all that behold it begin to mock him* (Luke 14:28-29). Therefore, we must count the cost as we make decisions. What are the consequences? Am I lined up with the word of God? Will my decision cause someone to sin? Will it have a negative influence in someone's life?

The directions we take will be determined by our relationship and fellowship with God. The turmoil comes when we want to do our will. The decision does not have to be bad but not God's will for us at that time. It is important to be in fellowship with God and to read and meditate on His word. Fellowship keeps us from being anxious and possibly making hasty and erroneous decisions.

I could not make a decision, initially, because I had to seek God and wait on Him for directions. Waiting can be hard, but it allows the anxiety to pass so we can make sound decisions. We must strive to be in God's time.

When uncertainties come, and they will; stop, seek God, wait for an answer, and proceed. Be careful not to be pressured into giving an immediate answer or of making an immediate decision. Pressure can cause us to make decisions that are not wise so it is imperative that we trust God for direction. God does not want us to be anxious for anything.

Let your conversation be without covetousness; and be content with such things as ye have: for he hath said, I will never leave thee, nor forsake thee. Hebrews 13:5

WHERE ARE YOU GOD?

Where are you God?
Why do you feel so far from me?
Why do I feel so alone?
Where are you God?

Have you forsaken me?
Have you turned from me?
I need you every step of the way.
Where are you God?

Don't leave me alone.
Don't turn from me.
I cannot survive from your glory.
Where are you God?

I cannot live apart from your love.
Shine on me dear God.
Don't leave me alone.
Where are you God?

"Where are you God" was written in desperation when I was going through difficulties in my personal life and in my ministry. I was not accomplishing what I felt I should in the ministry I was overseeing. Leadership had fallen because people left and current members would not commit to take leadership roles. The weight of the whole ministry was on my shoulders. People appointed to do things did not do them and did not communicate there intentions not to perform. There was also trouble in my personal life.

There were times when I could not hear the voice of God and I felt alone. I prayed and sought God but God seemingly was silent. God is never silent but I could not sense His presence. I know when I cannot hear God speaking it does not mean that He is silent. It means I missed what is being said or I need to exercise patience because God is working behind the scene. He is working and getting things in order to bring forth the answers to my prayer.

I had forgotten the scripture that says, *And this is the confidence that we have in him, that, if we ask any thing according to his will, he heareth us: And if we know that he hear us, whatsoever we ask, we know that we have the petitions that we desired of him* (1 John 5:14-15). God is working everything out according to His will and I wasted valuable time whining, crying, complaining, and worrying. The only good thing that came from those emotional binges was this poem that I am sharing with you. When I read this poem, it reminds me that God said, *Let your conversation be without covetousness; and be content with such things as ye have: for he hath said, I will never leave thee, nor forsake thee* (Hebrews 13:5). Now I know that God is always with me even when I cannot sense His presence. I must make sure that I have not drifted from God and His will.

When we think God has abandoned us, we feel alone and empty; but God is never away from us. The scriptures assures us that wherever we are God is there and that we cannot hide from God's presence (Psalm 139:7-18). This gives us confidence that nothing can happen to us without God's knowledge.

✝

We cannot hide from God's presence.

For God hath not given us the spirit of fear; but of power, and of love, and of a sound mind. 2 Timothy. 1:7

FEAR KEEPS CALLING ME

Fear of hurt.
I won't be hurt.
I won't let you close to me.
Listen!
Fear keeps calling me!

Fear of pain.
Don't walk out on me.
Don't leave me.
Listen!
Fear keeps calling me!

Fear of the unknown.
What's ahead for me?
Stop it! Stop it!
Listen!
Fear keeps calling me!

Fear! Fear!
Leave me alone.
I won't listen.
I want no parts of you.
Stop calling my name!

Fear keeps calling me is a poem I wrote while experiencing fear. The poem shows fear of persecution, rejection, and the unknown. All of us experience fear but we must not let it overwhelm us. God knew fear would come upon us as it came upon the people written about in the Bible. The phrase, "Fear not", is listed 63 times in the Bible. Each time the Bible lists "fear not" the next phrases are assurances that God is there, or that He will keep us. For example, *Be strong and of a good courage, fear not, nor be afraid of them: for the LORD thy God, he it is that doth go with thee; he will not fail thee, nor forsake thee* (Deuteronomy 31:6).

Fear is not of God. It is an evil spirit. Satan uses fear as a weapon to keep us from fulfilling the purpose God has for our lives. The scriptures says, *For God hath not given us the spirit of fear; but of power, and of love, and of a sound mind* (2 Timothy 1:7). We must stand on this scripture and make it active in our lives. Since fear is not of God, if we fear, then power, love and a sound mind is not in operation.

We cannot succumb to fear but must resist it and trust God. God wants us to have faith in Him believing that He will provide for us in every area of our lives. The Bible says, *"But without faith it is impossible to please him: for he that cometh to God must believe that he is, and that he is a rewarder of them that diligently seek him* (Hebrews 11:6).

We fear being hurt and vulnerable. This fear could be the result of traumatic experiences from the past--rejections from childhood and from persons we love. Rejection can cause us to erect walls to protect ourselves from being hurt and to prevent us from exposing how vulnerable we are. God wants us open and honest, but we cannot be open and honest when we hide behind walls built because of fear.

We fear the unknown. God does not reveal our total lives to us because He knows we cannot handle it. He knows we would be overwhelmed and that we would not trust Him. God allows us to face trials and tribulations as we are able to handle them. He wants us to trust and acknowledge Him so that we can handle our adversities through Him.

It is important that we trust God as we deal with fear. We cannot do anything about the inevitable except live a life that is holy unto the Lord. The scriptures says, *There is no fear in love; but perfect love casteth out fear: because fear hath torment. He that feareth is not made perfect in love* (1 John 4:18). God does not want His children living in torment because it hinders His plan for our lives. We must spend time with God and His word so we can perfect our love towards Him. We must trust God, enjoy life, and get rid of fear. God has the power to lead, guide, and protect us through any adversity.

The scripture, *Fear thou not; for I am with thee: be not dismayed; for I am thy God: I will strengthen thee; yea, I will help thee; yea, I will uphold thee with the right hand of my righteousness* (Isaiah 41:10), blesses me. Isaiah is prophesying to Judah that they are going to be taken into captivity by the Babylonians for 70 years but God will be with them. Even though they broke their

covenant with God, God wanted them to know that He chose
them and that he would not cast them away. Therefore,
they were not to fear or be dismayed. I believe this
message that Isaiah prophesied is for us today. This
encourages me and lets me know that God is with me and
not to fear even though I have made mistakes. FEAR
NOT!

✝

*God does not reveal our total lives to us
because He knows we cannot handle it*

Then Jesus called his disciples unto him, and said, I have compassion on the multitude, because they continue with me now three days, and have nothing to eat: and I will not send them away fasting, lest they faint in the way.   Matthew 15:32

COMPASSION! COMPASSION!

Compassion! Compassion!
Where are you?
I won't be like Sodom
Who did not care for the poor.
I won't be like Sodom
Who did not care for the fatherless.

Compassion! Compassion!
Where are you?
I won't be like Sodom
Who cared only for her pleasures.
I won't be like Sodom
Who was full of pride.

Compassion! compassion!
Where are you?

Sodom is a place known by most because of homosexuality, but according to the scriptures there were other problems, *Behold, this was the iniquity of thy sister Sodom, pride, fulness of bread, and abundance of idleness was in her and in her daughters, neither did she strengthen the hand of the poor and needy* (Ezekiel 16:49). Those in Sodom were a self-seeking people concerned only with their pleasures. They did not have compassion or mercy for others. They were prideful and greedy.

God wants us to love one another. He cannot tolerate indifference. God wants us to esteem others better than ourselves. The scripture says, *...but in lowliness of mind let each esteem other better than themselves. Look not every man on his own things, but every man also on the things of others. Let this mind be in you, which was also in Christ Jesus:* (Philippians 2:3b-5). We will not have compassion for others as we should if we are full of pride and selfishness. We will not be able to esteem others better than ourselves if we are self-centered. If we are in Christ Jesus, we must kill the flesh daily.

Jesus, during his earthly ministry, proved to be full of compassion. Throughout scripture we see evidence of His compassion as He heals and ministers to the poor and needy. He interacted with those who had needs--those who were halt, maimed, and down-trodden. Jesus brought hope to those who had none. We must have compassion because we are to be carbon copies of Jesus. We are to obey the scripture, *Let this mind be in you, which was also in Christ Jesus:* (Philippians 2:5). Indifference is not an attribute of Jesus neither should it be an attribute of ours. Each day we should walk in the commandments of God so we can have the mind and attributes of Jesus.

Compassion is born out of love. If compassion is lacking in us, we need to pray and ask God to teach us to love and have compassion for people. God is love and if we are born of Him we too must be love.

✝

Indifference is not an attribute of Jesus neither should it be an attribute of ours.

For the gifts and calling of God are without repentance.
Romans 11:29

DON'T SHUT ME OUT

I long to be your friend
But you closed the door.
I stood with hands extended
But there were no takers.
I looked around for someone
But no one was there.

Where did you go when I extended my hands?
Where did you go when I extended my heart?
Where did you go when I bared my soul?
Don't shut me out
Else I will close the door forever.

This poem was written at a time when I was deeply distressed. God had called me to preach and I was not answering the call. I was in a state of isolation but I did not understand why. There were times I was surrounded by people but isolated. My friends who at one time were close to me had scattered. My other "so called friends" were there but there was no connection. I was hurting and I was reaching out for help but it was as if no one was there. I did not fit anywhere--not even in my family.

I knew that if someone did not respond that I would build a wall around me that would never come down. I already had walls built because of the pain I experienced in my childhood. Now, I felt the walls extending and I was fighting to stop them from enclosing me.

God was working on me. He was separating me so I could hear Him but I wanted to connect with people. I did not want to hear the things He was saying. In fact, I acted as if nothing had changed. I was in denial. God moved everyone with whom I established a relationship. Those on the job, who became friends, left and went to other agencies.

I was in turmoil. I did not understand. I prayed, spent time with God, heard the things He said to me, and then ignored them. I continued to live a good and prosperous life. I excelled on the job, experienced new things but inwardly, I was hollow, isolated, and distressed.

I wasted years running from God and ignoring the call on my life, not realizing that God was not going to change

His mind.   Instead of running, I could have been developing my fellowship with God so that my life would be more anointed and fulfilled. All those years I tempted the hand of God!

Whatever assignment God has for us He will not change His mind, so we must move with diligence to do His will. Jonah is an example of a person running from an assignment God had given him. Jonah spent three days and three nights in the belly of a great fish. When Jonah repented, God allowed the fish to vomit him up on dry land. Afterwards, to perform the assignment God had given him Jonah went three-days journey in one day. We can avoid the Jonah syndrome--running from what God commands, going through pain because of disobedience, repenting from our decision, and then finally obeying God--if we obey God from the start.

Maybe you are isolated, sick, or hollow because you have been walking in disobedience to God. Let me help you--submit to God. Do not allow the desire you have for your life to fight against God's desire for your life. You cannot win.

✞

He was separating me so I could hear Him

*A soft answer turneth away wrath: but grievous words stir up
anger. Proverbs 15:1*

FRIENDSHIP DESTROYED

I thought the pain of betrayal was bad
Until I felt the pain of a friendship destroyed.
Long friendships are hard to keep
But a short talk can kill it all.

I thought the pain of betrayal was bad
Until I saw the hurt I caused.
Love pains are the worst
For it reaches out to destroy.

The tears I shed in my pain
Cannot repair the damage caused.
Forgiveness is a Christian's duty
Will you forgive me my remarks?

A valued friend betrayed me and in my pain I reacted in a harsh unfeeling way. This poem was written in my pain after many tears. The tears were because I realized I had destroyed a valuable friendship because I did not act in love. The soft words that turn away wrath were not spoken, only angry, unrelenting, and damaging words. The Bible says, *Be ye angry, and sin not: let not the sun go down upon your wrath:* (Ephesian 4:26). I violated this law because love was not shown.

I loved this person and the betrayal pierced my heart. The person and I had been friends for years with a friendship I thought would last forever. I did not have a clue that he would betray me. I did not remember the Psalm that says, *It is better to trust in the LORD than to put confidence in man* (Psalm 118:8). We put ourselves fully into friendships and we forget what Judas did to Jesus. We forget that he betrayed Jesus with a kiss. Jesus called Judas friend. If we would remember this, we would handle betrayals and not be devastated when it happens to us.

I released my friend that night from his betrayal, but the guilt I felt over my reaction and my harsh words kept me bound. I asked my friend's forgiveness and he forgave me instantly. I asked God's forgiveness and God forgave me; but, it took a while for me to forgive myself. Eventually, God let me know that I had overstepped my boundary because if He could forgive me, who was I that I could not forgive myself. I thank God for His forgiveness and for helping me to forgive myself. My mouth still gets me in trouble; but, I have learned to repent, ask for forgiveness, and forgive myself.

Then came Peter to him, and said, Lord, how oft shall my brother sin against me, and I forgive him? till seven times? Jesus saith unto him, I say not unto thee, Until seven times: but, Until seventy times seven. Matthew 18:21-22

LOVE PAINS

Love pains penetrate the core of the soul.
It demands attention to keep from destroying.
The hurt experienced cripples us unaware.
It causes one to retreat from reality.

Love pains demand retribution for relief.
It suffers longer when relief is denied.
It looks for an outlet to cast the hurt.
When none is found, it buries the pain.

Love pains fester and grow when buried.
It causes bitterness to penetrate the heart.
Bitterness cripples and grows.
It causes one to malfunction.

Love pains allow sufferers to often suffer long.
The hurt remains an open wound
Refreshed by memories often rehearsed.
When thoughts are not relinquished, they refuse to die.

Love pains given to the Lord
Helps to prevent hardening of the heart.
Release the injustice and let love continue
And live a life of joy and peace.

Love pains are the hardest pains to bear because the pain goes deep and it lasts longer. We are held hostage by the pain and if we are not careful, we will desire revenge. Revenge is a strategic plan satan uses to cause us not to forgive and to nurture the pain which can lead to bitterness. We can reach the point that retribution does not become a driving force even though it enters our mind. This is done by praying that God will help us not to nurse and rehearse the injustice, but to forgive. The desire for revenge is not God's plan for us as disciples of Christ Jesus, but the desire can be real.

God is love and He wants us to love despite the way we are treated. He knows that love makes us vulnerable and susceptible to be hurt, yet He still says, ...*Love one another*... (John 15:17). There is a trust that we have when we love someone; and when we feel betrayed, it shatters us. The first thing we do when we are hurt is retreat and build a wall around our heart to protect it from further abuse. We refuse to let that person or anyone else hurt us again. Despite the possibility of being hurt, we must love, be vulnerable, and put our hearts on the line over and over again. We have no choice because we are no longer our own but disciples of Christ Jesus.

As we experience pain, we must give it to the Lord to prevent becoming bitter and hardhearted. Bitterness will hinder our fellowship with God and mankind and will eventually affect the bones. We must guard our hearts so that we can walk in God's perfect will. Pain will remain in us as an open wound if we keep reminding ourselves of injustices done to us.

God has called us to walk in forgiveness. He has called us to forgive and release the person as many times as they hurt us. Look at Jesus and what the people He loved and came to save put Him through. Jesus was ridiculed, beaten, mocked, spat upon, threatened and finally crucified, yet He forgave. How many times have God had love pains because you betrayed Him? You told Him that you love Him, yet you go from one lover to another. As Jesus forgave, we must also release the pain and the person who wronged us so we can grab hold to the heart of God.

✝

How many times have God had love pains because you betrayed Him?

Likewise, ye younger, submit yourselves unto the elder. Yea, all of you be subject one to another, and be clothed with humility: for God resisteth the proud, and giveth grace to the humble. 1 Peter 5:5

GROWING OLD

You say the things of aging are unknown
And that fear lies at the door.
You say changes are hard to bear,
Yet you try to succeed.
I say, you are aging gracefully.

"Growing Old" was written as I considered the changes we go through as we age. We are not going to remain young and our bodies are not going to remain smooth and supple. Life involves changes and we must flow with the changes or we will be miserable.

Let us not be shallow creatures that only look at the outer appearance but make sure our hearts are filled with love. Aging is a blessing from the Lord and should be done with grace. God has a plan for us and if we are still alive at whatever age, it is a blessing. We should seek God to find His purpose and plan for us so that we can walk in obedience to that which he has ordained.

We must not allow fear to operate in our lives. God kept us through our young and foolish days and He is able to keep us in our latter days. God does not change. Trust Him for new mercies each day and remember that goodness and mercy are assigned to us.

Sometimes we allow the cruel and insensitive behavior of the immature to make us feel useless and unnecessary. We cannot worry about the opinions and behavior of others but follow what God allows. Those who are not old must learn to respect the aged and not condemn or treat them with disrespect or disdain. Remember, if we are blessed to become senior citizens, how we treat or have treated others is how we will be treated. We must grow old gracefully and trust God to meet all our needs. We must also remember that we were never in control of our lives–God was.

Brethren, I count not myself to have apprehended: but this one thing I do, forgetting those things which are behind, and reaching forth unto those things which are before, I press toward the mark for the prize of the high calling of God in Christ Jesus. Philippians 3:13-14

KILLING THE PAST

The closer you get to me
The farther away you become.
The more you love me
The more I need your love.
As time passes,
You look hopefully to me.
I cannot receive your love
Nor can I give you love
Until I kill the pain of the past.

Many of us must kill the hurts of the past in order to become whole. The wounds of the past left open and festering can hinder our freedom to love, to experience the wonderful things in life, and to be ourselves. The past is not necessarily a life of crime and immorality but could be a life of pain inflicted by others.

This poem refers to my life. A life of pain, rejection, and fear. My past has held me in bondage most of my life and still does at times. I wrote this poem because I believe others also go through trauma in their childhood, carry it into their adult life, and never understand why they are the way they are.

When people seek to build an intimate relationship with me, I back away. I feel suffocated and will often say or do something to kill the friendship in order to push the person away. I did not understand why I reacted that way until God showed me that I was fighting for survival. It was an unconscious effort to protect myself from pain that can be inflicted by those who are close to you.

I have three good friends that have loved me enough to push pass the barriers and have gotten close to me. Every now and then I still try to push them away but they ignore me. They don't understand me, but they love me enough to stay.

I asked God one day in my quiet time, "Why am I the way I am?" God who is loving and ready to commune with us when given a chance, explained. He said that those who were close to me were the ones who hurt me as a child. He showed me I could not trust people to become close to me for fear they would hurt me as those that had done so in the past. God took me back to my childhood and showed me the things that traumatized me. He showed me the abuse, the hatred, and the pain. He showed me so much that I cried as if my heart would break. He showed me a 10 year old girl who felt alone and traumatized as she went through torture and abuse by those who should have been loving, nurturing, and comforting her. A little girl who had been taken from one who loved her and thrown into a cruel world of faces, bodies, and pain.

When God showed me my past, I cried for that 10 year old defenseless girl. I cried heart-wrenching tears. The memory was so painful that I called my sister-cousin and told her about the things that happened to me at the age of 10. I continued to cry and she listened and consoled me.

There were experiences before the age of 10 that left lasting impressions on my life but none as traumatic as the things I experienced at 10 years old. The things that happened to me at that age were major in shaping my present condition. The pain is subsiding. Hopefully, by sharing my pain it will lead to a full recovery. Until I kill the hurts of the past, I cannot be as intimate with people as God requires of me. God wants me open and vulnerable with people and He says I will be hurt. God also said that He can heal all wounds.

I have released those who offended me but I have not released the memory and pain of the assaults. I know that God will heal, deliver, and make me whole.

Paul says, *...forgetting those things which are behind, and reaching forth unto those things which are before, I press toward the mark for the prize of the high calling of God in Christ Jesus* (Philippians 3:13-14). That is my desire. As I started writing this scripture, a weight fell from me and I felt a lightness. I believe this is my healing. I intend to forget the anguish of the past and press toward the mark for the prize of the high calling of God in Christ Jesus. I am a victor in Christ Jesus and I am killing all offenses of my past.

I am no longer in bondage to the enemy regarding the pain of my past. When satan attempts to bring the pain back, I have learned to lean on scriptures such as: *Finally, brethren, whatsoever things are true, whatsoever things are honest, whatsoever things are just, whatsoever things are pure, whatsoever things are lovely, whatsoever things are of good report; if there be any virtue, and if there be any praise, think on these things* (Philippians 4:8*)*; and, *And we know that all things work together for good to them that love God, to them who are the called according to his purpose* (Romans 8:28*)*.

The offended often becomes the offender because of the past. Those I have offended because of what happened to me, forgive me. I pray you can forgive me as I have forgiven myself and those who offended me. My acts may not have been as cruel as those inflicted upon me but if they caused pain, mental anguish, or shortcomings, I still stand guilty of cruelty. I did not understand the cruelty that often came out of me until I heard a preacher say, "Hurting people hurt people". Please forgive me! You too must kill past offenses as I am killing past offenses.

Then he which had received the one talent came and said, Lord, I knew thee that thou art an hard man, reaping where thou hast not sown, and gathering where thou hast not strawed: And I was afraid, and went and hid thy talent in the earth: lo, there thou hast that is thine.   Matthew 25:24-25

THE CEMETERY

The cemetery I visited today
A place of quiet solitude
A place of loss, pain, and loneliness
A place where dreams are buried.

The cemetery I visited today
Reinforces the fact that life is worth living
Death leaves dreams unfilled
And buries them in the cemetery.

The cemetery I visited today
Secluded and hidden from life
Many dead by their own hand
Many killed by the hatred of others.

The cemetery I visited today
Lonely, sad, quiet and dead
A place of lost love ones
Who are now memories of the hearts.

This poem was written after going with my husband to the grave site of a relative. I felt an unusual quietness in that place. It was the same quietness I experienced when I went home after the death of my father. There was an emptiness and loneliness that I could not explain.

I thought of the people buried in the cemetery--young and old, strong and weak, drifters and dreamers whose time in this life was ended. What was in those people that could have benefitted us and was now buried? Some lived their lives to the fullest and did everything they desired, but what about those who were weak, fearful, and unmotivated? What fears prevented them from sharing what God placed in them for us? Was there a book, a song, a sermon, a poem, an invention, a thought? What great thing did they take to the grave unfinished?

What was the cause of their death? How many could not face life and committed suicide? How many ingested drugs into their bodies trying to kill the pain that was caused by an uncaring parent, spouse, friend, church member or pastor? How many were killed because of hate? It is important to treat people with love and respect. Each person is different and we do not know the extent our negative actions can have on them.

The scripture for this poem, Matthew 25:24-25, deals with money but the principle is for whatever God gives us. He gives us gifts and talents to use to the fullest. The gifts are also to be used to love, encourage, and comfort one another.

On your next visit to the cemetery, think of families, friends, and others that are buried there. Do not just think about what they took to the grave, but what did we give them, and what legacy will we leave for those who will be left when we are buried in the cemetery?

✝

What Legacy will we leave?

✝
GOD'S LOVE IS EVERLASTING!

If ye abide in me, and my words abide in you, ye shall ask what ye will, and it shall be done unto you. John 15:7

LET GO AND LET GOD

When you have no control,
Why worry and torture yourself?
Let go and let God.

When life overwhelms you,
Before you go under.
Let go and let God.

When all hope is gone,
Do not surrender to pressure.
Let go and let God.

One of the most enlightening things I learned in the last 10 years that still blesses me is that I do not have control over anything. It is all God. I cannot get up in the morning unless God allows it. I cannot think unless God allows it. I can stand with my arms around my daughter protecting her and she can die or be killed at that moment. I have no control; but God has everything in control. I must give my concerns to God; in other words, let go and let God.

The scripture that freed me is, *I am the vine, ye are the branches: He that abideth in me, and I in him, the same bringeth forth much fruit: for without me ye can do nothing* (John 15:5). The Word says that without Him I can do nothing. The Word also says, *If ye abide in me, and my words abide in you, ye shall ask what ye will, and it shall be done unto you* (John 15:7). Jesus gave me a blank check to get my needs met. With these kind of promises, I would be remiss not to let go and allow God to work out my concerns.

There are times in our lives when calamities happen and we feel overwhelmed. This is not a time to surrender and go under. It is a time to read the scripture that says, *Casting all your care upon him; for he careth for you* (1 Peter 5:7). The scriptures also say, *Be careful for nothing; but in every thing by prayer and supplication with thanksgiving let your requests be made known unto God* (Philippians 4:6).

God promised Abraham and Sarah a child and instead of trusting and waiting on God to do what He promised,

Sarah lost hope. Sarah did not let go and let God. Instead, Sarah gave Abraham her hand maiden, Hagar, to wife so that she could have a baby through Hagar. Hagar was a slave and slaves did not own anything. When Hagar became pregnant and when she had her son, Ishmael, problems started. We cause problems when we try to do God's job. Ishmael was not the promise God had for Abraham and Sarah. Isaac was the promised son and he was to come through the womb of Sarah.

Sarah surrendered to the pressure of her desire and of time lost. She stopped trusting God to bring life to her dead womb and worked to counterfeit the promise God made concerning her. What God promises, God also performs. God said He will supply all our needs. LET HIM!

✟

I cannot get up in the morning unless God allows it.

For I came down from heaven, not to do mine own will, but the will of him that sent me. John 6:38

SLOW ME DOWN LORD

When I would rush ahead of you to do my will,
Slow me down Lord.
When I would run and plan before seeking you,
Slow me down Lord.

When I would rush around always in a hurry
Slow me down Lord.
When I fly through life, rushing in and out,
Slow me down Lord. Slow me down!

Readers, I am sure you do not have this problem of rushing through life never slowing down long enough to get a word from God except at your convenience. When you stop, you tell God what is going on, what you want to do for Him, His church, His people, but never allow God to talk to you. Then you wonder, "seems as if I have missed something". Yes, you missed the voice of God directing you.

God calls us to spend time with Him and it is not only for us to talk but also to listen. God is not looking for a chatterbox but an open heart to listen. Prayer is, also, a time for God to pour Himself into us, to build us, and to cause us to grow in Him. God is wisdom and if we slow down and listen to Him, we will have more time for Him and those things He ordains. We are still to pray for people and set aside time just for God. Set aside time for intimacy between Him and us where we love Him and allow Him to love us and share with us.

We have misplaced our priorities when God is not first. When we forget to put God into our schedule or when we do not allow Him sufficient time, we have problems. When we give God top priority and allow Him to set our time, we will have success. Jesus came from Heaven to do God's will. We should be doing God's will also instead of rushing around to do our will. We cannot spend too much time with God. If our day is full to capacity and we give God quality time, He will redeem the time or give us the time we need. A three hour meeting can be finished in an hour because God can work situations out before the meeting. Slow down and try Him.

I am the LORD: that is my name: and my glory will I not give to another, neither my praise to graven images. Isaiah 42:8

TO GOD BE THE GLORY

When we were sick, Lord,
You healed us.
When we were distressed,
You comforted us.
When we were lost,
You reached out and saved us.
When we felt unloved,
You loved us.
To you God be the glory,
Nothing we did, Lord, just you.

When we were confused, Lord,
You sent the Word to ease our troubled minds.
When we needed help with our children,
You counseled us.
When our mates' love dwindled,
You touched their hearts and our love grew.
When we were lonely,
You filled the void with your Word.
To you God be the glory.

When we were filthy and shameful,
You picked us up and cleansed our souls.
When we were hungry,
You moved upon the heart of man to feed us.

When we were destitute,
You miraculously provided shelter for us.
When we were jobless and the rent was due,
You provided before we asked.
O God, the glory is thine.

When we were surrounded by corruption and hatred,
You built a shield around us.
When we were surrounded by jealousy and envy,
You showed us their hearts.
When our enemy would slay us,
You hid us in your bosom thus protecting us.
To you God be the glory,
It was not us but your grace, Lord, your grace.
TO GOD BE THE GLORY.

God states in his word that He will not share His glory with another. I believe the sooner we realize that without God we can do nothing, the sooner we can stop taking God's glory. Every good and perfect gift comes from above. It is God's grace that allows wonderful things to happen. We must also realize that it is God's grace and mercy that keeps us while we are in the midst of trials and tribulations. We do not have the ability to keep ourselves, only God does.

If we are not careful, we will take God's glory and God says He will not share His glory. When we come out of trials, we sometimes say, think, and act as if we did it. We did nothing, it was all God. Nebuchadnezzar is an example of a man who unwittingly took God's glory (Daniel 4:29-32). Nebuchadnezzar took credit for building Babylon to be great by the might of his power and, consequently, God's wrath fell upon him. God took the kingdom from him and drove him out to dwell with the beast of the field. It was not until Nebuchadnezzar lifted up his eyes to heaven, that his understanding returned unto him. Later Nebuchadnezzar acknowledged God and gave praises unto Him. He was restored into his kingdom.

King Herod is another example of one who took God's glory. The Lord smote King Herod because he allowed the people to look upon him as a god. The people praised Herod, *"...saying, It is the voice of a god, and not of a man...* (Acts 12:21-23). He took God's glory and the angel of the Lord smote him. Do not let the praise of others put you in jeopardy of being judged by God because you decided to take His Glory.

We must remember in our deliverance and success that it was nothing we did but it was God working in our lives. The distresses, trials, and tribulations have been overcome by God's mighty hand because we ask, submit to, and trust in Jesus. Thank God for deliverance, grace, mercy, and goodness because it was all Him. DO NOT TAKE GOD'S GLORY!

✝

It is God's grace
that allows wonderful things to happen.

Great is the LORD, and greatly to be praised; and his greatness is unsearchable. Psalm 145:3

RESTING IN THE ARMS OF GOD

The warm glow of a summer morning
Does not compare to the glow found in the arms of God.
The security of a guarded house
Does not compare with the security of His embrace.
The comfort of a mother's arms
Does not compare with the comfort of His caress.
The strength of a father's grip
Does not compare with the strength of His hand.

I am resting in the arms of God because
Nothing compares to His greatness.

We need to feel secure and true security is obtained through connecting with our Savior and Lord Christ Jesus. Our connection with Jesus allows us to know with all our might that He is in control. The connection allows us to know that nothing is going to happen unless He allows it and if He allows it, He will make a way of escape. If He chooses not to change the situation, we know that He will give us grace to go through. Jesus told Paul that, *my grace is sufficient for thee: for my strength is made perfect in weakness...* (2 Corinthians12:9).

There is no security in the promises of man, nor in a job, but security is in God. We know He will perform what He says. *The Lord is not slack concerning His promises...* (2 Peter 3:9).

God is a God that cannot lie and He continuously shows Himself strong. Knowing that His caress, His embrace, and His strength is like no other, gives us hope, joy, and peace. This kind of security comes only from God. I marvel at God because of who He is, all that He has and what He can do. Who would not serve a god who thinks good toward them continuously. *Many, O LORD my God, are thy wonderful works which thou hast done, and thy thoughts which are to us-ward: they cannot be reckoned up in order unto thee: if I would declare and speak of them, they are more than can be numbered* (Psalm 40:5). *For I know the thoughts that I think toward you, saith the LORD, thoughts of peace, and not of evil, to give you an expected end* (Jeremiah 29:11). God wants us to look for good things and for Him to give us an expected end.

The more I know about God the greater my faith and my love is towards Him! How can I not love someone who loves me unconditionally? How can I not love someone whose thoughts are of peace toward me and who has made me for Himself and for his pleasure?

Resting in the arms of God is a safe haven for those who seek refuge--refuge from our enemies and refuge from satan and his attacks. Resting in His arms gives us peace in any situation. Sleepless nights become peaceful nights of secured rest. Let us trust Jesus and surrender all to Him for He offers a place of rest.

✞

How can I not love someone who loves me unconditionally?

Render therefore to all their dues: tribute to whom tribute is due;
custom to whom custom; fear to whom fear; honour to whom honour.
Romans 13:7

AN INSPIRATION

To do better, to grow stronger,
To overcome life's defeating perceptions,
These are life's greatest desires.

To know where you were
And see where God has brought you
Is an inspiration.

To step in the forefront with grace,
To achieve dreams and reach for more,
That is an inspiration.

To see the cannot's in life,
Overcome them, and press forward,
These are things that inspire and push.

To accomplish the things you fear,
To step in waters untested.
What an inspiration.

An inspiration causes one to do better and
To strive for mastery.
You are an inspiration.

An inspiration was written for a young lady that had a desire to teach. She started in Church School and God elevated her to not only teaching in Church School, but retreats, and a radio ministry with her husband. She submitted her will and desire to the Lord and stepped outside of herself. Now the Lord is using her in a mighty way.

We must trust God and follow His lead. We have no idea where God is leading us. The question is, will we follow blindly as Abraham when God called him to leave his country and go where he did not know or will we assess the situation and follow our thoughts or our desires?

I honored this young lady because it was inspiring to see someone who was unassuming and unsure of herself stand boldly and proclaim the gospel in church school, retreats, on the radio and in conferences.

We can do all things through Christ who strengthens us. We must come to a place in our lives where we allow the Holy Spirit to lead and guide us to do God's will. We have dreams and desires but often fail to accomplish them because we fear stepping into untested waters, or we fear failure. I believe desires never tried is failure.

I believe we should inspire others and ourselves to do and do better; to reach and reach higher; to dream and dream more. We must trust God and reach outside of ourselves for "the more". It is "the more" that God wants for us and from us.

This is the day which the LORD hath made; we will rejoice and be glad in it.   Psalm 118:24

LOOKING AHEAD

Today I stood and watched life pass by
As I had many times before.
I stood on the outskirts, not a participant,
But an onlooker.

I realize now that looking ahead
Is not a passive, but an active thing.
I realize that I must become a participant in life.
I must make my mark and fulfill my destiny.

The potentials in me will never be known
If I allow life to pass and not be a participant.
All that I am must be developed
To bring out the potentials within me.

Potentials that lie dormant helps no one.
I must allow God to order my steps that
I may grow in grace and favor.
God will not have me ignorant of His ways.

The days must end of never participating and
Of existing secure in my safety zone.
I must grow to please my God
For stagnation is a nasty smell in His nostrils.

Looking ahead shows expectation, trust and hope.
Looking ahead shows expectation of things to come.
It shows trust and hope in an eternal God.
I must look ahead to receive all His blessings.

Looking ahead is what makes us
Dependent upon an omnipotent God.
I must participate, I must grow,
I must develop my potentials.

I will look ahead to fulfill my destiny
Knowing God will be pleased.
I will look ahead with expectation
For the day of our Lord's return.

Looking ahead may mean following a dream that God has birthed in us of reaching heights never uttered but trusting God to bring them to pass.

Life is too short to always be a spectator and never a participator. Being a spectator requires no effort, but being a participator means dreaming and making those dreams come true. As the poem says, by looking ahead it shows expectation, trust, and hope. Going through life without expectations hinders progress. Being a participator causes you to dream and grow because a participator is always seeking for new horizons. God wants us to look ahead, to reach, and to trust Him. If we expect nothing, we will receive nothing. By being a spectator, it shows that we are afraid to move. The fear may be of failure. We certainly cannot fail in an area we have never tried but we cannot win in that area either.

God gives us life to enjoy and that means being a participator. God wants us to rejoice in each day and be glad knowing that He gave us the day.

Many dreams have been taken to the grave because people were afraid to look ahead, and with faith, step into the unknown. We must seek God for the truth about who we are and what He wants for us. We must stop listening to dream killers who do not know the potentials God has placed in us. We must step out in faith knowing that God is ordering our steps. Do not let your life end never having lived, and do not cheat us out of what God gave you for us. Live, trust God, follow your dreams, and fulfill your destiny. LOOK AHEAD!

ROADWAY TO SUCCESS

Our success in life is not determined by what we have, or what we have accomplished, but by our relationship and fellowship with Christ Jesus. If we acquire throughout life as many houses, as much money, and as much recognition as we want or need, we will still be empty. The rich young ruler was seeking, but went away sorrowful because he was still looking for things and not the man, Christ Jesus. He did not need more things, he needed a relationship with Jesus. The rich young ruler could not get pass the things he had in life, his success. They were more of a treasure to him than Jesus (Matthew 19:16-22). Does this parable fit you?

The road to success is to let go of our lives, and our situations, and let God do His will in, through, and by us. After all, He made us with a purpose and our destiny will be as He has purposed. Conflicts, mountain top experiences, and the valleys, will come, but true success is in Christ Jesus. Receive Jesus in your life. He is waiting for you to surrender to Him.

Success lies in our obedience to God's word. Joshua says, *This book of the law shall not depart out of thy mouth; but thou shalt meditate therein day and night, that thou mayest observe to do according to all that is written therein: for then thou shalt make thy way prosperous, and then thou shalt have good success* (Joshua 1:8). Find your RoadWay to Success--let go and let God have control of your life.

✝

Success lies in our obedience to God's word.

SCRIPTURES

Finding Joy in Your Seasons
Ecclesiastes 3:1-8
Nehemiah 8:10
Psalm 30:5
1 Corinthians 10:13
Ephesians 2:7
Colossians 3:17
Philippians 4:4
Hebrews 12:2
1 John 5:14

Uncertainty
Proverbs 3:5-6
Luke 14:28-29

Where are you God?
John 5:14-15
Hebrews 13:5
Matthew 28:20
Psalm 139:7-12

Fear Keeps Calling Me
2 Timothy 1:7
Deuteronomy 31:6
1 John 4:18
Hebrews 11:6
Proverbs 3:5
Isaiah 41:9-10

Compassion! Compassion!
Matthew 15:32
Philippians 2:3-4
Ezekiel 16:49

Don't Shut Me Out
Romans 11:29
James 2:7
Jonah 1-3

Friendship Destroyed
Proverbs 15:1
Psalm 118:8
Matthew 18:21-22
Ephesians 4:26

Love Pains
1 Samuel 1:10
Matthew 18:21-22
John 15:17
1 Corinthians 13
Hebrews 12:5
1 John 4:8
1 John 1:9

Growing Old
Proverbs 3:5
Romans 3:8
1 Peter 5:5
1 John 3:11
1 John 4:7

Killing the Past
Philippians 3:13-14
Philippians 4:8
Matthew 18:21-22
Romans 8:28
1 Corinthians 15:57
Exodus 15:26

The Cemetery
Matthew 25:24-25
Romans 12
1 Corinthians 12
1 Corinthians 14

Let Go and Let God
John 15:7
John 15:5
Genesis 16 - 21
1 Peter 5:7
Philippians 4:6

Slow Me Down Lord
John 6:38

To God be the Glory
John 15:5
Isaiah 42:8
Isaiah 48:11
Daniel 4:29-32
Acts 12:21-33

Resting in the Arms of God
Exodus 15:2
Psalm 18:2
Psalm 19:14
Psalm 40:5
Jeremiah 29:11
Romans 4:21
2 Corinthians 12:9
Ephesians 1:5
Titus 1:2
2 Peter 3:9

An Inspiration
Romans 13:7
Proverbs 3:5

Looking Ahead
Psalm 118:24
Hebrews 11:6
2 Samuel 22:3
Psalm 7:1

RoadWay to Success
Matthew 19:16-22
Joshua 1:8
John 1:12

TEACHING SESSIONS

Letting go of the Past and Rebuilding our Lives
Prayer: An Encounter with God
Come See A Man
Evangelism: A Lifestyle
The Book of Genesis
The Gospel of Matthew
The Book of 1ˢᵗ John
A Mind to Work - Nehemiah Chapters 1 - 6
Pursuing a Deeper Relationship with God

ORDER INFORMATION

To order this book, fill out the requested information below:

Name_____

Address _____

State _____Zip Code_____

Telephone Numbers_____

Quantity _____

Cost of Book: $7.95

Allow Maryland sales tax = 5%

Shipping and handling charges - $2.50 in the USA

PAY WITH CHECKS OR MONEY ORDERS

Please make checks or money orders payable to Georgia E. Wells.

Send order and payment to:
Resurrection Life Publications
Attn: Georgia E. Wells
P.O. Box 1644
Temple Hills, MD 20757